Dirty Talk

An Easy To Follow Manual For Using Only Dirty Words In
Your Sexual Interactions, Building Confidence, And More

*(Having A Sex Conversation Mastery Without Feeling
Foolish)*

Jimmy Barber

TABLE OF CONTENT

The Influence Of Living A Life Apart From Relationships 1

What Ladies Look For In A Man 9

Developing Self-Belief 20

Busting Communal Sexual Myths 38

Process Of Sexual Communication 55

It Might Be Frightening And Nerve-Wracking To Talk To Girls. 106

How To Be A Bad Boy That Women Want (Not A Dick) 120

Talk About Sex And Puberty Begins At Home 150

The Influence Of Living A Life Apart From Relationships

Avoid the temptation to get on your phone like a hungry cheetah when that special guy always starts ringing. Alternatively, let it ring and give him a call back when you're free.

Accepting your own fabulousness, being independent, and avoiding becoming overly attached to your partner are the keys to winning a man over and keeping him interested.

As we all know, guys hate to be ignored, but they also need space. So go ahead and live your life, hang out with your girlfriends, and give him the cold shoulder now and then. Unbelievably, a lot of guys enjoy the thrill of a good pursuit. If they see you having the time of your life, they will pursue you even more ferociously.

They are enamored with busy ladies who have many fascinating things going on in their lives. It intensifies their allure, rendering you completely unstoppable in their view.

The Secret to Entertaining in a Mysterious Way

Imagine yourself on an exciting first date, with the almost irresistible want to tell your charming suitor everything about your life. Hold on, sweetie, though! He might run for the hills if you reveal too much too soon. An attractive woman who retains her mystique is what guys admire.

They are drawn to the mysterious charm of a woman whose thoughts are enticingly concealed, which compels them to don their detective caps and carefully try to discover the mysteries that lie within.

Men are eager to explore the depths of your fascinating psyche and won't let up until they figure it out. Thus, rather than presenting your life story to him polishedly, pique his interest gradually with tidbits of knowledge.

Make him curious about your secrets so he will beg for more. You become alluring in disclosing just enough to keep him interested while retaining your air of mystery.

Hello, my love. The secret is in the art of balancing. Thus, embrace your inner mystery and make him want to delve into the depths of your alluring spirit. He'll be following your every move in this complex game of disclosure and concealment, wanting to piece together the fascinating mystery that is you.

I have to admit that I have had my fair share of firsthand encounters with being a curiously seductive woman. Permit me to guide you through a few of these fascinating incidents that have influenced my perception of this work of art.

I still vividly recall a masquerade event I attended a few years ago. I chose to embrace my mystique while I dressed in a beautiful gown. Presenting a mysterious smile and exuding confidence, I discovered that I was encircled by curious suitors keen to decipher the mystery that was me. I delighted in the ability to pique people's curiosity with my quiet looks and thought-provoking talks.

Another time, I went on a solitary adventure to a charming beach town. Observing the puzzled looks of other travelers, I couldn't help but stroll along the beach with the breeze softly ruffling my hair. I left them guessing about the depths of my psyche and the hidden secrets that lurked within, projecting a calm and enigmatic aura. The secret to being enigmaticly seductive was ingrained in my nature and went beyond my outward appearance.

I remember a fascinating dinner gathering where vibrant discussions were prevalent regarding intellectual attraction. I participated in conversations that straddled the topics of philosophy, art, and the secrets of the cosmos with a sparkle in my eye and a hunger for knowledge. People around me were enthralled by my blend of wit, wisdom, and a hint of mystery, and they were left wanting more of the intriguing depths that remained hidden beneath the surface.

However, being enigmatic and intriguing is not just reserved for formal occasions or glitzy environments. I've understood the value of subtlety and understated charm, even in the most straightforward situations. Be it a quick smile shared with a stranger at a coffee shop or a glance that piques someone's interest in passing, mastering the skill of being enigmatic yet attractive has enhanced the fabric of my daily existence.

I've learned from these firsthand encounters that being a strangely attractive woman is a form of art that knows no bounds. It's about living true to who you are, developing an air of mystery, and leaving people wanting more. It requires carefully balancing assurance, nuance, and a hint of mystery.

What Ladies Look For In A Man

Before discussing the real date, you must recognize the differences between men and women.

Women are more emotional, whereas males are more sensible and practical. This implies that women base their decisions on their current emotional state. Thus, rationally persuading a woman that you are her best option throughout the date will not produce the desired outcome.

Rather, you must commit yourself to putting her at ease and experiencing strong emotions with her.

Women want a man to be a man, not to beg for their attention, to have an interesting life, to be able to take charge of them and dominate them, to be accountable for his actions, to be proactive and active, and most importantly, to be able to say no when he doesn't want to comply with them in every situation.

Women naturally look for security in their spouses; they want a man who can care for them and is confident.

Being reckless, impulsive, or intimidating others are not characteristics of self-confidence. Having self-confidence entails knowing what you want and having faith in your skills.

You are responsible for making decisions as a man, just as a woman is free to accept or reject.

Remember that for a woman, deciding is the only thing that matters—whether it's right or not. When you make decisions for her or both of them, you come across as a responsible, mature, dependable, determined man who understands what he wants.

When it comes to women, it's your responsibility to initiate contact, strike up a conversation, ask for her phone number, call her to set up a date, decide what to do when you see her again, and, in the end, initiate the kiss. Whoa!

Though there are certain exceptions, no woman in the world will take care of everything for you.

You can't expect a woman to tell you what to do or when to do it. She will attempt to convey her intentions implicitly, particularly through body language, but you will still need to take action, even if it appears hazardous.

Let's return to why the traditional "take out for dinner" is not the ideal first date now that you better understand men's and women's roles in society.

A lot of men want to look well on their first date. Giving them presents and accolades, showcasing their wealth, or bragging about their social standing.

You have to understand that if you try to flatter a woman and don't pass up the opportunity to flaunt your wealth (dress elegantly, drive her home in a fancy car, take her to the most upscale restaurant in town), she will think that you are only doing this to get her attention because your personality isn't strong enough to win her over.

You don't need to be a millionaire to woo a beautiful woman; the innate attraction between men and women stems from specific social dynamics unaffected by financial status. Why, in your opinion, do the ladies find themselves drawn to the workplace colleague, the tennis instructor, or the village animator? Is it because these men asked them to a posh restaurant for dinner?

In addition, if you tend to flaunt your material belongings rather than your thoughts and character when interacting with women, you may encounter financially motivated ladies eager to take advantage of your generosity. They usually won't give you what you want as long as you can afford them, and they'll "take it long" to make the most of this circumstance.

CONSIDER: Would you rather a woman be interested in what you can buy her than in you?

You will know precisely what to do when you go out with a woman if you know exactly what it takes to pique her attention and arouse her sexual desire in him.

What occurs in most situations?

In general, males believe, "Now I take her to a classy restaurant, and she will feel indebted to me, to return the favorand to show me her gratitude, she will be more inclined to have sex with me."

This small-minded attempt to make her feel deserving of your favor won't accomplish the intended goals. You might get a kiss or a future release promise, at most. She is doing this to make amends and to be by her conscience, not because she wants you.

Let's look at how to ask a woman out now that you better understand what she wants from a man and the pitfalls to watch out for.

When speaking dirty, what should you say?

Though most girls find it amusing, very few use foul language when having sex with their partners or husbands. Finding the right words to use is girls' biggest issue in this area, but I have a fix. I've gathered some advice from a user forum that might help you get started and have a nasty conversation.

1. Don't be overly polite while asking your partner what he wants you to do or how he wants you to do it. It all comes down to being upfront, honest, and free. Don't be scared to say things like, "My juicy wet pussy is just punching for you," or "Fuck me, dad."

You have no idea how this chat will make him feel. It takes practice, like anything else in a relationship, even though it might initially seem strange.

2. Start with the basics. Every time I have sex with my boyfriend, we start from the fundamentals, so it feels like a brand-new experience.

I'll ask him what he would do to me if he got his hands on me, and I won't answer any questions about what I wear or whether I'm wearing lingerie. It could take some time. Recall that the cycle of dirty language begins even before seduction occurs, and it does not begin in bed.

3. Simply and logically ask him to do what you would like him to accomplish. You can tell him to tighten or kiss you, for instance, but remember to speak out. Men are creatures of challenge, and they will challenge themselves to do nothing

that would increase their self-esteem or satisfy their desires. However, if he does something that makes you feel good, don't forget to give credit where credit is due.

4. When you describe your feelings for him, picture what you mean. This is the emotional content of sex, so when you engage in dirty talk, concentrate on it. But it's up to you to express your feelings to him through words and deeds because he might not be able to see or hear them.

Tell him about your back trembling, the sensation of your firm cock in your cunt, and how wonderful it is to have your tongue in your mouth—everything contributes to what might be thought of as sophisticated dirty speech techniques during intercourse.

5. do you intend to be thematic when you use foul language? If you participate, this is even more awesome. For instance, if you were a woman and he was a man, you would engage in dirty language along the lines of "Excuse me, sir. Would you mind sticking your enormous member into my vagina?

However, the topic revolves around the initial phases of pregnancy, so it would be ideal if you could maintain it throughout the session. The most frequent subjects include prostitutes and how to get what you want, pirates, teachers and students, instructors and cheerleaders, and others.

Speaking nasty is only one of the personal lessons two people learn over time; there is no set script to follow. When you figure out the first problem, you should know what to do, how, and what your man wants to hear or respond to.

With any luck, these five suggestions will enable you to carry on having satisfying but unpleasant sex and, in the end, fortify your bond.

Developing Self-Belief

Developing your confidence is crucial to drawing in ladies and creating enduring partnerships. Being confident means having faith in oneself and moving forward with one's plans. When confident, we are more willing to take chances, speak clearly, and form closer relationships. Self-esteem is the foundation of confidence, the conviction in one's value and potential. A person with a high sense of self-worth is more inclined to take calculated chances, trust in themselves, and communicate clearly. It's critical to confront negative ideas and attitudes and concentrate on your accomplishments and talents to increase your sense of self-worth.

How to Increase Your Self-Belief

1. Visualization is one method of boosting confidence. The process of forming mental pictures of oneself accomplishing a goal is known as visualization. One might begin to trust in

one's ability and take action toward reaching one's goals by envisioning oneself as confident.

2. Taking care of your appearance is crucial to developing confidence. This entails caring for your health, dressing nicely, and practicing cleanliness. You are more likely to feel confident and move toward your goals when you feel and look well.

3. It's also critical to develop assertiveness, which is the capacity to defend your rights and effectively express yourself. Being assertive can help you become more confident in social settings and improve your communication ability.

4. Another excellent strategy for boosting confidence is to be in the company of upbeat and encouraging individuals. We are more inclined to believe in ourselves and take action toward reaching our objectives when surrounded by people who support and believe in us.

The Significance of Self-Belief in Grabbing Women

Being confident is essential for attracting women because it's a quality many find appealing. Communicating successfully and possessing a strong self-worth are important components of confidence. A confident man is more inclined to approach girls, start a discussion, and leave a positive impression. A man is likelier to hold a conversation and make the woman laugh if he is confident in himself and his skills. Being confident affects how we interact with others and how they see us, which makes it a crucial component of attraction. We are more likely to be viewed as appealing and desired when we exude confidence. Our mannerisms, tone of voice, and body language reflect our confidence level. Demonstrating interest and making physical touch might be facilitated by confidence. It can be challenging to express interest or make physical contact when one lacks confidence, making starting a discussion challenging. Our confidence level might also influence how we display ourselves in various contexts. For instance, someone who exudes confidence is more likely to feel at ease and at ease in social settings, which can enhance their attractiveness and desirability.

Anxiety might be useful for dealing with rejection. Being rejected is a normal aspect of dating, and when we are secure in ourselves, we can accept it and go on.

The Value of Self-Belief

It is crucial to remember that confidence can manifest itself in several ways. Being gregarious and boisterous is not always a prerequisite for confidence. Some people could be more reserved and use more subdued means to convey confidence. For instance, introverted people could demonstrate their confidence by their knowledge, abilities, or intelligence. It's critical to realize that confidence is a multifaceted trait not exclusive to any personality type.

The fact that confidence is a trait that can be enhanced and grown is another crucial feature. One can learn and grow confidence via experience; it is not an innate trait.

Finally, it's critical to remember that developing confidence is a continuous process rather than a one-time occurrence. Things outside oneself, such as stress, criticism, and rejection, can impact confidence. To be ready for the highs and lows of dating and relationships, it is crucial to continuously work on gaining and sustaining confidence.

Chapter 2: Importance of sex in maintaining relationships

The Value of Sexual Activity in Partnerships

Can a relationship endure without having sex? Indeed. Needs do not necessarily involve having sex. On the other hand, it could be quite important in a fulfilling, healthy relationship.

Everybody views the importance of sex in a different way. Some people think that engaging in sexual activity is essential. Some people think some types of intimacy and connection are more important than others.

For the following reasons, you may think that sex matters in a relationship:

Being closer to your lover, showing your love for them, enjoying sex, wanting to make a family, feeling confident and beautiful, relieving tension

Frequent sexual activity has been shown to have an impact on an individual's overall well-being. Sexual relations are usually linked to greater affection. When a couple is more affectionate with one other, they are more likely to have sex more frequently.

Sex can be an essential part of a relationship, even though having sex less frequently does not necessarily mean that your relationship is any less pleasant.

For interested parties, there are several health benefits to bonding through sexual activity. Discover the value of having sex in a relationship, regardless of whether you're polyamorous or monogamous.

Over time, sexual activity can and often does change. However, this does not mean that the rate of sexual activity must drop indefinitely. Sex can be just as wonderful now as it was when you first fell in love, is the answer to that question. Closeness and sex can develop in a relationship with time and maturity. It might just require a little more work.

There are a lot of ways to spice up your sex life. It can be helpful to think about the non-sexual aspects of your relationship.

The greatest sex organ is often described as the space between the ears. If there isn't a stronger emotional bond or improved communication, having more sex will probably not lead to long-term relationship changes. Stress management is another crucial element of a healthy sexual life.

If you keep waiting for your level of desire to catch up to your partner's, you could be waiting for a very long time. Rather, talk to people about what you want and work toward a mutually agreeable solution.

● You may adjust the frequency of your intercourse throughout your relationship. Speaking with your spouse might improve your sexual pleasure and build your bond.

When partners have sex, talk, and have physical touch, they compromise better and speak more honestly. Superior. In a way, consenting, happy, and mutually consented sexual activity fills up the holes and gaps in relationships.

However, the benefits of sex extend beyond the mind and feelings. It offers a special set of health advantages.

Chapter 3: Select Books That Are Age-Correct

Overview

Various materials about sex education have been made available online in recent years. It's challenging to bring up the topic of sex with your kids. But now that there are age-appropriate sex books available, you may discuss sex with your kids without feeling too awkward.

As your child gets older, it's normal for them to have questions about sex, and they need honest answers. Studies show that age-appropriate literature can help you start a conversation with your child about sex.

Books can also be a last resort if the discussion is a bust.

Some benefits of reading books that are age-appropriate, artistically created, and specifically targeted for your child are listed below.

The Advantages of Reading Books About Aging

The first step in having a meaningful conversation with your child about birds and bees is to read some of the age-appropriate books designed to help you have those conversations. The best age-appropriate novels are readily accessible this year, so parents need not worry about finding them.

These books will assist your child in learning more about the subjects they are interested in learning about in the actual world of sex. Talking to your youngster about sexuality and sex might be challenging at first.

It will, however, get better and simpler with time and practice.

You can choose the greatest books for your child's age group because most age-appropriate sex novels are meant for a wide age range. You can be sure that your child will learn a lot from these age-appropriate sex books and that the majority of their sex-related inquiries will have correct and honest answers.

There are various approaches to starting a conversation with your child about sex, and these books will enable you to quickly and simply explain and mentor them.

When it comes to sex issues in particular, the majority of teenagers consider their parents to be the most influential individuals in their lives.

As a parent, it is your responsibility to support and manage your child's sexuality and sex. When the term "sexuality" is mentioned, what immediately comes to mind?

Sexuality encompasses the workings of both male and female bodies, various forms of partnerships, reproduction, human growth, prevention of STDs and pregnancy, and sexual behavior.

Some parents intend to talk to their kids about sex for months because they think they can teach them everything about it at once. Conversely, parents will get angry if the conversation does not go as planned. The conversation you have with your child about sex and sexuality should last a lifetime.

Talking to your child as soon as possible is essential to preventing doubt and inquiry. This is the best time to start a conversation with your child when their curiosity shows. During the talk, you'll see that your youngster and you are becoming more trustworthy and courteous, which you will like.

Encourage your young children to read age-appropriate books so they may become familiar with the names of their bodily parts. It's important to keep the conversation about sex with your child age-appropriate. As a result, they will be more equipped to handle the subject and understand the difficulties associated with sex and sexuality.

Being accessible and receptive is the finest thing you can do as a parent, particularly when your child wants to discuss delicate subjects like sex. Age-appropriate books can be given to your youngster.

Age-appropriate material is readily available, so you won't have any trouble teaching your child the significant components of sex.

Busting Communal Sexual Myths

In this chapter, a few common myths about sex beliefs will be discussed.

1. Men desire constant sexual relations.

We don't desire constant sex, is our response. Regretfully, it seems that women likewise think that men must always be able to desire whatever they want. It's quite hard for a man to turn down promised sex because women usually think it's "wrong" and make you look unmanly. Everything is alright. Like women, guys only want sex when they want it. The issue is that, frequently, they are unable to distinguish between the sex they want and the sex they don't until after it has been had. Most men, though, need to do better than that.

2. Sex is just sex to males.

Sex is a form of validation.

Men constantly battle with self-doubt. They attempt to ignore it, to hide it behind obnoxious arrogance, and occasionally, they attempt to break the negative patterns that cause them to feel self-conscious. Men try to hide their inadequacies out of fear that women won't find them appealing if they don't seem confident in themselves. It might be more ideal.

But sometimes, it's best to silence your inner critic and listen to the adults. A collapse follows the orgasmic sensation in a woman's arms. That's the finest one.

3. One factor is power.

While the dominance myth isn't entirely true, it's not horrifying. Men desire you to be lost in an exuberant sea of fury, madness, and forgetting who you are. They want to be the ones to take away your self-control, and they also want you to lose any sense of self-control. But in actuality, everyone wins; therefore, power is irrelevant.

4. Men grow aloof from a lack of empathy

The reason we're apart is because we're concerned.

The ultimate litmus test for a man is his sexual aptitude. Success, athletic ability, and witty banter aside, if they aren't deadly in the sack, they have failed miserably as men. Men think there are many different ways they could fail. It takes far too long, or it ends too quickly. They may be overly severe or overly gentle. Men fear that if they display too much emotion, you'll think they're crazy about them or, worse, that they'll turn you off entirely. The worst feeling is knowing that they won't let you leave.

While some women experience orgasms solely from physical pleasure, many others have more complex experiences. We don't know, but it could be physical stimulation, emotions of safety and danger, a loss of power and control, crossing our fingers, and hoping for the best.

Guys don't want their ladies telling their friends how horrible they are in bed; instead, they want them to have fun. It might be nerve-wracking. Because of this, men will sometimes act indifferent, which may become habitual. On the other hand, we do care a great deal.

5. Men Are Very Aware of Sex Issues: Women Most Likely Understand Sex Issues Better Than We Do

Usually, when men engage in physical acts of love, they cannot look at themselves in the mirror. Women, however, get a firsthand account of what guys are like when they're having sex. If you want to know what sex means to guys, try to put your prejudices aside and listen.

6. All men are the same when it comes to sex.

The reason is that each of us is different.

This is the biggest secret since it's not a secret. It is common knowledge that there is no infallible way to comprehend men. To understand a man sexually, you must have sex with him. Numerous examples.Because it could be awkward for both genders to discuss sexual expectations.

7. Men are more driven by sexual desire than women.

False is the response. Women can have strong sexual desires as well, provided they engage in appropriate mental and physical foreplay. We women love having sex. We may require a little more emotional affinity at first, but once we get going, well, you get the picture. Several studies indicate that women attain their second sexual peak in their late 30s, which may lead to an increase in libido and sex desires.

8. You Need An Orgasm To Have Good Sex.

Response: UNTRUE. Though it may seem hard to imagine, you and your spouse can still enjoy yourself without dealing with nonstop "OHs" and "YES." Doctor Kristen Mark (of sex) says that concentrating on having fulfilling sex with your spouse instead of merely "getting off" will enhance the quality of your relationship. According to a recent study, the duration of a sexual encounter may be a more appropriate method to classify sex than its frequency. They want to make your spouse orgasm, which can get in the way of savoring the good times.

9. All love sex.

False is the response. It's important to remember this fallacy when you go on dates. Not everyone has a pleasant and healthy perspective on sex. Some people could be desirous of having sex, but they struggle to enjoy it because of an unpleasant or traumatic past. In this case, exercising enormous patience, respect, and compassion is imperative. In situations when there has been repeated sexual trauma, it may be beneficial to see a couples therapist or sex therapist. Rebuilding a positive relationship with sex will be facilitated by therapy.

Section Two

LOVE, TRUST, AND RESPECT

This is the most important part of the book. It's simple to understand, but it can be difficult to put into practice: only have sex with individuals you love, respect, and trust. This is a message that this country missed on the path to sexual enlightenment, and I know that some readers, if not most of them, will think me foolish. Since sexual pleasure has supplanted any remotely similar emotional connection, our children stand to lose the most. I get depressed talking to teenagers who not only have trouble identifying true love, respect, and trust but who also don't think that these things have to be present in a relationship before they can have sex. Likely, kids haven't had deep discussions with their parents about the importance of these three elements. Have you helped your child understand what love, respect, and trust are all about? Have you tried to instill in your child, whether they are five, ten, or fifteen, the importance of building a mutually loving, respectful, and trusting relationship with your life partner? It seems obvious that we would want our kids to look for these traits when choosing who to have sex with if we want them to value accountability, respect for others, dependability and honesty, and empathy for others.

The Power of the Big Three

It's important to start teaching your children at a young age how having these three things in a relationship reduces the risk of unwanted pregnancy, sexual assault (like date rape), STDs, and other negative consequences of physical contact. When you have total mutual respect, trust, and genuine love with someone, you never have to worry about them trying to purposefully hurt you, trick you, or bring you down. Think about how many people would mistreat their spouse in general, act carelessly and not wear a condom during sex, hide their HIV or STD status, and sexually abuse others. At the same time, in a relationship, they cheat on their partner. This knowledge is really important. However, if you genuinely love, respect, and trust someone, such negative things won't occur.

In my conversations, I came across many parents who value these three fundamental ideas for their kids. They want their kids to grow up to be responsible adults. They want their children to be trustworthy, honest, and compassionate, and they also want them to respect other people. Parents also want their children to form relationships with individuals who share the same core values, hoping and expecting their children to be treated as they would others. But many of them say that would be unrealistic and too high of an expectation when I ask them whether they would want their children to only have sex when they truly loved, respected, and trusted someone. Many of them contend that having a fulfilling sexual relationship is perfectly acceptable.

What makes two people wanting to have sex so controversial? Why do we feel compelled to teach our kids that they can't engage in sexual activity or enjoy something enjoyable until they are completely infatuated and have the respect and trust of the person they will be spending it with? I've been questioned by parents, "Why should I make my kids live up to those standards if I didn't? It's also quite antiquated. When I tell parents to teach their kids to apply my criteria of love, respect, and trust to determine when it's right for sex, some parents feel I'm going too far.

Instead, let us study reality. Might you be worried that someone you can trust, who truly loves you, and who you can be sure of might try to harm you on purpose? That you could have been intentionally infected with HIV or another STD by this person? That this person might just be using you for their sexual pleasure? that this person would desert you if you became pregnant? Or that they would try to take advantage of you sexually, like making you have sex when you didn't want to? Every time, the answer is no. Think about this. If we all waited to have sex until we were completely in love, respected, and trusted with one another, we could avoid a lot of the health problems caused by risky sexual behavior. There would be a decrease in sexual assault, unintended pregnancies, and STDs like HIV. Regretfully, though, our society has struggled for decades to obtain control over these grave health dangers among youth. Adolescents participating in risky sexual behaviors are among the top six causes of sickness and death in the United States today.

For now, let's put the explicit material aside. Consider how important the big three are to the longevity and success of any relationship. Think about how crucial it is to teach our kids that genuine love, respect, and trust build a bond between two people that cannot be broken. Everything else in a relationship, such as physical attractiveness, financial stability, fulfilling sex, sharing music tastes, and other relationship-related aspects, is secondary to developing respect and trust. Together, they build the strongest bonds with another human being when paired with true love, which can only come from morally aligned beliefs, compassion for others, and kindness. Disagreements are inevitable in any committed, loving relationship, but they are easier to resolve when love, respect, and trust exist.

Along the way, we'll also provide useful information about how to evaluate and manage interpersonal interactions, the significance of contraception—particularly the use of condoms—and how to make key decisions about our children's sexual behavior. Stated differently, our goal is to prepare kids for as many real-world situations as possible so that when they're adults and do occasionally engage in sexual activity with someone else who doesn't have the three primary ingredients, they'll do so in a way that greatly reduces their risks.

Process Of Sexual Communication

The sharing of thoughts, feelings, and information about a sexual connection between two people is known as intimate communication. It's a process that requires both participants in the relationship and vocal and nonverbal communication.

In terms of sexual communication, verbal exchange is crucial. It entails talking about expectations, feelings, and desires. It's critical to have honest and open communication with your partner and to be sensitive to their needs and desires. It's crucial to share any worries or difficulties and consider and respect one another's boundaries.

An essential component of sexual communication is nonverbal communication. This can include physical contact, facial emotions, and body language. Gestures, posture, and eye contact are examples of body language. Expressions on the face can convey happiness or displeasure. Communication can also occur through physical touch. Hugging, kissing, and touching are examples of this.

It is possible to convey wants, create sexual tension, and set the tone using both verbal and nonverbal communication. It's critical to understand your partner's comfort zone and ensure that both of you participate in the process.

The process of sexual communication is dynamic and ever-changing. It's critical to consider your partner's requirements and to be willing to talk about and consider novel concepts. Couples can have a happy and rewarding sexual connection with each other if they communicate openly and courteously.

Talking about fantasies and trying out various sexual acts can also be included in conversations about sex. Both lovers may find sex more delightful and satisfying as a result of this.

To put it briefly, having healthy and consensual sexual relationships requires an open conversation about sex. It promotes safety, fosters trust, and enhances the pleasure of sex. To have the greatest possible sexual encounter, make sure to talk about consent, birth control, STDs, and other subjects.

Subcultures of men and women

A long-standing social and cultural phenomenon is the subculture of men and women who are sexually active. It encompasses a variety of sex- and sexuality-related actions, viewpoints, and customs. Several social movements, including the feminist and LGBTQ rights movements, have had an impact on both male and female sexual subcultures.

A "subculture" is a discrete set of values, beliefs, and behavioral patterns that emerge inside a broader culture. Common conventions, beliefs, and lifestyles define subcultures. This encompasses attitudes and views about sex, gender roles, sexual orientation, and the body in the context of male and female sexual subcultures.

The term "female sexual subculture" refers to the range of gender-specific sex and sexuality-related behaviors, attitudes, and practices. This covers subjects like the autonomy and enjoyment of female sexuality as well as female sexual expression. It also covers the usage of other sexual gear, including sex toys like vibrators and dildos.

The term "male sexual subculture" refers to a range of gender-specific actions, viewpoints, and customs surrounding sex and sexuality. Topics, including male sexual expression, autonomy, and pleasure, are included in this. It also covers the usage of various sexual gear and sex toys like fleshlights and prostate massagers.

The sexual subculture of men and women is a complicated and dynamic phenomenon that social, religious, and legal factors have influenced. Understanding that the sexual subcultures of men and women are separate and shouldn't be confused is crucial. In addition, it is important to honor and appreciate the sexual subcultures of both men and women.

Understanding our culture and civilization requires an exploration of the complexity of human sexuality. Gender roles, cultural standards, and legal limits are just a few of the variables that might influence sexual communication. Furthermore, the development of male and female sexual subcultures might be influenced by these circumstances. For instance, while some cultural standards are more acceptable in some nations, others may be more common in others. This may result in various attitudes and behaviors among various subcultures related to sexuality. It's also critical to acknowledge that learning about and comprehending the subtle differences across various sexual subcultures can aid in our comprehension of the larger social environment surrounding sexuality.

Fundamental model of communication

Encoding is the process of turning a concept or idea into a message that the recipient can understand. Usually, words, symbols, or other means of communication are used to accomplish this.

A communication method that eschews encoding and decoding is known as bypassing. This is accomplished by transmitting a message straight to the recipient without first encoding it so the recipient can comprehend it.

Interpreting an encoded message conveyed to a recipient is called decoding. This requires interpreting the language, symbols, or other communication methods used to convey the message.

The answer the recipient provides after deciphering the message is known as feedback. It is crucial to communication because it enables the sender to determine whether the message was understood correctly, and if not, it permits additional clarification and/or modification.

To put it briefly, feedback, encoding, bypassing, and decoding are all crucial aspects of communication. Effective communication requires each of these elements.

Tips for nonverbal communication

1. Make eye contact: Eye contact with your partner is an easy yet powerful nonverbal communication technique. Maintaining eye contact with your

spouse can help you better comprehend their sentiments and is a sign of connection and trust.

2. Body language: One excellent method of nonverbal communication is to be aware of both your and your partner's body language. For instance, leaning in, touching, or holding hands might convey attention or affection.

3. Expressions on the face: Using facial expressions to communicate nonverbally is quite effective. Expressions like smiles and frowns might help you understand how your partner feels.

4. Speaking is not as crucial as listening nonverbally.

5. Touch: Using touch to convey nonverbal messages can be quite effective. It's acceptable to touch your partner's hand, shoulder, or arm to show comfort or affection.

Chapter 3: Presenting It to Your Spouse

It's acceptable for many people to want to add more pleasure and excitement to their sexual interactions. However, it could backfire if done poorly. Wanting things to change in the bedroom is insufficient. Acceptance or rejection of the change may depend on how you present it.

After learning about the advantages of dirty language and how our psychological makeup supports it, let's speak about how to introduce it to your partner in a safe manner. This procedure is especially important for several reasons. That might be the case:

● Neither of you has ever attempted to talk filthy.

● Your spouse is the sort to avoid sexual contact.

● The sexual enthusiasm you both had as younger lovers has been sapped by daily pressure.

Whatever the situation, it's not difficult to learn how to bring up or bring up the subject of dirty language in a relationship. However, it is important to approach it cautiously because it involves personal beliefs or boundaries, emotions and feelings might get out of control, and moods can be abruptly destroyed.

A Comprehensive Guide to Enrolling Your Partner

Proceed cautiously.

It's not necessary to begin with really explicit or graphic language. If you come out as overly assertive right immediately, you can irritate your partner. Even worse, your partner might believe you are having an affair if you suddenly alter your sexual behavior. Proceed cautiously. Start by gently making tempting comments to your companion. You might choose from a list of basic yet seductive statements in the Beginner portion of Chapter 5 of this book, such as "You look so sexy tonight."

Proceed from there and work your way up to riskier approaches to sexual expression. However, make sure you constantly assess how receptive your spouse is. You can terrify them by bombarding them with a series of dirty phrases.

Expand on the prior momentum.

Starting your naughty discussion in the bedroom is usually preferable unless you are bashful. Before you start messaging your spouse when they're at work or aren't with you, let them grow used to hearing you say inappropriate things. Consider how weird it would be if someone you've been dating or married to for a while suddenly sent you a lewd text when they aren't even able to use one sultry phrase in the bedroom. Strange, huh? You can be extra flirtatious, groan more, and generally show your spouse that you are coming out of your shyness in the bedroom, even if you are too nervous to start practicing your sex talks face-to-face. It won't seem too odd if you send them something spooky the next day as a follow-up.

The main goal is to change their perception of you in a comfortable environment and then to build on that impression. The next thing to do is to continue flirting with them in public, on the phone, in texts, and during talks. You don't have to use foul language or other obscenities when you flirt with them.

Just use body language or provocative wording. You will quickly learn that they are amenable to mild profanity. You can take more daring actions, like saying something highly inappropriate in their ears in public if you're feeling particularly confident. For instance, ask them to meet you in the restaurant restroom in a whisper. If you choose to subtly give them your undies and say, "I'll be in the bathroom... waiting," you have sent a pretty explicit message even though you did not use any foul language!

Discover what they prefer.

When it comes to discussing sex, what does your spouse want? Regretfully, there's no way to find out this without doing many tests or, if you're feeling particularly bold, just asking them. Some partners like their indiscretions mixed with their innocence. Saying something like, "I've been fantasizing about you inside me all day, but I'm too shy to let it show," can make them more receptive. Typically, this implies that the partner in question likes to take the lead during sexual activities. If that is the case, you will have to adopt the role of the submissive. Some partners adore vulgar statements such as, "Come give it to me like a sex-starved creature!" This kind of partner could be more adept at playing the neutral or submissive position. They are receptive to your suggestions.

It's also crucial to modify your sex talk to fit your partner's fantasies, interests, occupation, or even recent events in your life together. Say something like, "Come play me like your favorite notes on the guitar," or "Use your moist lips to paint all over my body," if your partner is an artist or plays the guitar. Alternatively, if they recently closed a big deal, made a ton of money, or got promoted at work, you could say something like, "Fuck me like the richest dude/chick on the block," "Make love to me like a (new position) would," or "Show me how a successful agent makes love."

Find out what your spouse enjoys talking about during sex and come up with a plan that works for both of you.
Be sincere.
This one is possibly the most important mindset to assist your partner in tolerating your trash talk. Responding to internal or external sexual triggers is the main theme of dirty talk. Consider it to be more of a reaction than an action. You are answering or reacting to an actual emotion that you are experiencing. Dirty language is essentially a linguistic manifestation of your most liberated, self-assured, and natural sexual self. It's simple to be yourself and speak up about what represents your true self when you approach erotic or sex talk from this

angle. Unless you are a talented actor or actress, putting on an act is a certain way to ruin your partner's mood. Say only what you want, feel like saying, and are at ease saying. Say it out loud if you want to make passionate love. And convey a strong desire for it. Choose any term (gritty or suggestive) that best expresses your feelings.

As an illustration:

- I want to have a sexual encounter with you that you will never forget.
- I desire intense, passionate love from you.
- I want you to give me the little bitch treatment.

You don't have to say things that make you uncomfortable since your partner will find out quickly, which will seem strange. But if you're introducing or restarting nasty talk to your spouse, following this chapter's suggestions and beginning with gentler words and phrases is best.

Being sexually aggressive is not required.

It's not necessary to be overtly sexually suggestive or obscene in your language to arouse your partner's interest in passionate sex. Use those phrases if your partner feels comfortable using stronger language and enjoys acting aggressively toward you. However, you shouldn't automatically assume they would enjoy foul language because they frequently act aggressively in bed. Start gently and see how they react. You can tell by their response whether or not they are amenable to more vulgar language.

For couples in committed relationships, having a one-night stand is not the same as having sexual interactions. A partner you met at a wild party or in a bar would not mind if you engaged in really offensive conversations and acted sexually aggressively. Ultimately, they will eliminate you within a few minutes or hours. However, taking things slowly with a long-term partner is important until you figure out when their tolerance peaks.

3.

HOW TO SPICE THINGS UP WITHOUT FEELING FILTHY: DIRTY TALK

W

When you hear the term "dirty talk," what immediately comes to mind? Does it remind you of any sultry moments from a pornographic film? Maybe it's so cheesy you can't imagine putting it in your bedroom. Perhaps it's so naughty that it induces feelings of naughtiness in you. You know, the conversation that makes your heart race and your partner's ears perk up.

Even the most accepting people have their limits when it comes to discussing dirty things. It's normal to initially feel a little nervous. However, isn't that what adds to the excitement? Sex wouldn't be as exciting if it was all sunshine and rainbows.

Yes, the explicit language in those pornographic movies may be a bit excessive and ridiculous. However, the vulgar language this book will teach you is anything but tasteless. It's elegant, alluring, and—dare we say it—very hot. To be sultry in bed, you don't have to compete with a porn actress who reads scripts. Hey, darling, real life is the real deal!

We're not claiming that you will suddenly become a sexpot, though. You can't become an expert nasty talker overnight. But don't worry, we'll go slowly and start with the fundamentals. You'll whisper lovely nothings to your spouse, and they'll beg for more before you know it.

It's also critical to keep in mind that having healthy sexual connections involves more than just foul conversation. There are many alternative ways to establish a close, personal connection with your spouse if you don't feel secure or at ease doing it.

My parents warned me about the value of honoring my body and my sexuality when I was about twelve. They discussed with me the risks associated with having sex too young and without the appropriate protection. They also forewarned me about the harmful consequences of pornography and how it can skew my understanding of what constitutes healthy sexuality.

I was a little awkward and ashamed to talk to my parents about it. But retrospect, I see how crucial that conversation with me was for them. I was able to make knowledgeable decisions regarding my sexual health and cultivate a positive attitude toward sex as a result.

I now realize, as an adult, how important it is to be open and communicate about sex. I've discovered that using derogatory language to improve intimacy and establish trust with a spouse may be quite effective. However, I also understand that handling it delicately and respectfully is critical, considering my partner's boundaries and preferences.

I feel empowered to make healthy and informed decisions about my sexuality and to explore it in a way that is secure and fulfilling for me and my partner because of my parents' stern talk.

Lastly, remember to enjoy yourself while doing it! Don't take dirty conversation too seriously; it may be a fun and exciting way to liven things up in the bedroom. Unwind, let go of your guard, and savor the journey. Who knows where you might end up with it?

Section Two

Go outside and explore your wild side.

Demonstrating your mischief when you're just starting a relationship is challenging. You have a thousand questions racing through your mind. If not, what will she think of it? You can, however, gently reveal your naughty side to a woman without frightening her away. Here's how to accomplish it.

setting up

It's not always necessary to express your thoughts aloud. You can show her your naughty side with some acting skills if you're familiar with each other and have had sex in the past. This calls for creativity on your part. To let her know what you want to do with her, you could, for instance, bring candles and rose petals into the bedroom or cook while nude. His thoughts will not stop, and he will not stop wondering what you plan to do to him.

regain command

To demonstrate naughty love to a woman in the bedroom, be assertive and take charge. But before you do anything, find out if she likes being bossed around and controlled in bed. If not, it can backfire. For some ladies, it's seductive. However, be cautious not to exert too much influence over it. Perhaps she might enjoy it in bed but not outside.

Make fun of her.

Rest comfortably in your sleeping quarters. Avoid being overt. Examine and draw objects on her erogenous regions. Tease her in the areas that she is most sensitive to touch, such as her inner thighs and ears. Keep your hands off it. Allow me to implore you to interact with her. He puts her on top of him, holds on to her till she begs, and then gives in to her desires after a short while. She can be teased outside of your bedroom as well. All you need to do is be inventive. talk impolitely

During their bedroom time, couples typically don't chat much about anything. You ought to be, though. It can be seductive. Tell her how much you desire her or what you want to do to her while speaking in a seductive, sensual voice. It will reveal your naughty side to a woman. One of the safest methods to demonstrate your meanness without hurting her is to do this.

Remove it from your sleeping quarters.

Your bedroom doesn't have to be the center of attention. There are a lot of spaces in a house that you may use. It can also be exciting to take a shower with her, watch a sexy movie on the couch late at night, or catch her cooking at the kitchen counter. You can make filthy love to a woman even in public if you two are even more daring. Play pretend

It's an age-old method of displaying your naughty side to a woman. Choose the appropriate role—such as a shy cook with a mischievous mistress or a naughty boss—and then incorporate some mischief into it. It might expose the relationship's necessary ugliness.

playing with toys

Adult toys are a terrific way to introduce some naughtiness into your relationship, while some couples find them a little kinky. Men's and women's toys are available. Increases your level of enjoyment. It's not your birthday, so you may give it to him instead.

Ask him before you do anything. Ask her whether she wants to test or feels safe using it, even if you surprise her with a toy. Verify if she approves of the plans you have for her. If he doesn't give your relationship his all, your bad side will damage it.

It's typical for couples to find it difficult to keep their hands off one another while their relationship is just getting started. However, learning how to explore closeness with your spouse that may continue for years is crucial if you want to take your relationship to the next level.

Being emotionally and sexually connected to your partner is crucial for any relationship. This is something that both spouses must actively work on. Does "intimacy" come to mind when you consider entering a sexual relationship? Do you view sex as a means of self-expression, love, or feelings? You're not alone if you find yourself saying "no."

Most people's expectations in a physical relationship and their actual real experiences diverge greatly. These are a few of the greatest methods to investigate and enhance your connection in the bedroom.

1. Establish a relationship

The relationship or tie between partners is crucial. Both must establish a strong bond with their bodies. Many of us are prevented from maintaining a comprehensive and regular self-care regimen by stressful everyday tasks, including work, housework, bill payments, meal preparation, etc.

Consequently, many of us spend less time getting to know, appreciate, and embrace our bodies. Regretfully, these all have a detrimental effect on our sexual lives. It is impossible to have an intimate and enjoyable sexual relationship with someone else if we are unable to create an intimate and enjoyable relationship with ourselves.

We must make space to experience, explore, and appreciate our bodies. Couples may be able to discuss needs, wants, and what will completely fulfill them in this way.

Furthermore, you don't have to choose love to prevent loneliness. You must develop the habit of spending time alone. Recognize that you are safe and secure in the relationship's boundaries. You may feel content, whole, and at ease as a result.

2. Transform the commonplace into the exceptional

People learn commonalities and take alternative actions to avoid similar problems when their romantic feelings wane. The trick could be as simple as adding a little "coziness" to your routine to make it remarkable. Open your heart to your lover and divulge your deepest fears and secrets.

Happiness is something that unites people, and it's what keeps a pair together. One aspect of this happiness is the desire to be in the company of happy people. Make an effort to develop true intimacy with your spouse. Sharing everything with your partner makes a special place in their lives, which can also bring out the best in you. Many of you look for romance and unwavering closeness to compensate for the voids in your lives, yet this can lead to pain. Establish a close, loving friendship with few expectations.

3. Masturbation between the two parties

There is nothing more intimate than witnessing a spouse enjoy. It's something that every relationship should try: mutual masturbation.

The greatest sexologists promote this as the most personal practice. It's extremely easy; just settle into a comfortable bed and have your spouse sit beside you to observe. Maintaining eye contact with your spouse is crucial in this situation.

This is because people find it more entertaining and desire more when they see it. Should you pay attention to their level of pressure, where they touch, how they touch, or whether they use lubricant when your lover professes their love?

It can provide you with amazing suggestions for improving your partner's satisfaction. You can read sex stories on eroticatale.com to heighten your desire for your spouse throughout this seduction session.

4. strolls at night

It's not necessary to limit your sexual exploration of closeness to your spouse; taking a walk at night while holding hands can also deepen your bond. You may feel closer to your lover as a result.

When you go for a long walk with your spouse and hold hands at the end of the day, it's incredibly attractive and good. It might assist couples in expending extra energy following a demanding day.

You can appreciate the peace of nature or have a deep and meaningful talk with your significant other while taking a lengthy walk. A deeper, more emotional connection—which is crucial for sexual intimacy—can result from these late-night excursions.

5. Discuss about sex

Remember that you don't need to be bashful around your significant other. By being open and honest about sex, you can increase the intimacy in your relationship to the greatest extent possible.

Take a seat back, unwind, and discuss your desired sexual life with your significant other. Tell him what makes you feel attracted to him. Talk to him/her about the bottlenecks you want to investigate. Share your favorite sex-related memories to date.

Discussing sex can be difficult at times. Open discussions regarding it are uncommon. However, experts say it can be unsettling to discuss sexual urges amid physical contact. After that, you have to schedule a day to discuss your sexual wants for a week.

You can include activities you like to do during sex with your spouse, new things you're willing to attempt, activities you want to do during sex with your sweetheart, and much more.

Physical intimacy can also refer to your partner's touch and proximity; it is not just about having sex. Therefore, take the above advice from the sexual gurus and step up your intimacy game right now if you've been longing to explore and increase intimacy in your relationship.

The word tantra, which refers to transcending the human into a higher level of being through spiritual enlightenment, is loosely translated from Sanskrit as "that which liberates."

Many people mistakenly believe that tantric ideologies are focused on sexual activities. Still, their goal is to elevate humans from the mundane frequency of life into the divine form, where peace and clarity can be found.

Tantra has a physical origin, but its practices eventually transcend into the psychic and psycho-spiritual realms and merge with the Supreme Being. Tantra places more emphasis on doing than on understanding. Therefore, applying these liberating processes is just as important as simply being aware of them.

Tantra is a set of exercises that opens your mind and ultimately leads to freedom from the gloom of an unfulfilled life. An individual who follows the tantric path is called a tantric.

Most men suffer from internal rather than exterior illnesses, and by engaging in tantric practices, one may be able to transcend their restrictions and unite with the divine.

Tantra allows one to transcend mental boundaries, get over mental encumbrances, and experience the wisdom of the Absolute.

Humans have always been curious about their place in the natural world from birth. If all you use is reason and reasoning, it is hard to understand where you are. Thus, tantra assists all souls in searching for the reality of their being. It leads to a whole human being by embracing all aspects of life.

According to the tantric worldview, Shiva and Shakti are the two energies that created the universe. Ultimately, these energies are the same; nevertheless, the feminine power, Shakti, also known as Prakriti, represents pure energy, and the male force, Shiva, also known as Purusha, represents pure consciousness.

These forces symbolize the male and female energies in every person and should not be mistaken for something distinct, such as two distinct places occupied by the male and female forms. We all have a masculine and a feminine form, and tantric practices may assist us in bringing these energies together so that we might transcend everyday reality.

Ordinary people rarely see the unity of life because Shiva's pure universal consciousness is constrained in the physical world and becomes the individual or the "I." This restriction fosters the growth of the ego, which occurs when we fail to see ourselves as universal beings and instead define ourselves in terms of "I." "I am this or that" keeps us apart from our unity, which is our eternal identity.

The feminine force is likewise limited in the physical world, which prevents us from fully appreciating the universe's limitless pure energy. Until a person overcomes their ego and the need to see the world from their perspective, the feminine force, or Shakti, remains dormant.

We remain asleep, imprisoned in the dream world, as long as we maintain our selfish "I" perspective of the world. We shall always be in a condition of sleep as long as we believe the world is an illusion.

The term "kundalini" refers to the dormant feminine force. This energy is greatly misinterpreted; individuals mistakenly believe that a tiny tingling in their spine indicates the awakening of this energy. Recognize that awakening the kundalini feminine force requires purifying your mind, nerve system, and physical body first. You must leave behind an egotistical view of reality to activate Kundalini. Since bringing the Kundalini Shakti into balance is not simple, very few people have attempted to do so.

Yoga is a systematic and progressive process that purifies the body and awakens the dormant Shakti energy to merge with the Shiva awareness. The dormant Kundalini energy is awakened and ascends to the topmost chakra during Shiva and Shakti's reunion.

You may harmonize your mind, body, and energy with yoga, letting go of your anxieties, fears, and limits as you ascend into a universal state of awareness that manifests your everlasting identity.

The concept of Shiva and Shakti permeates all substances in the world, both living and nonliving, and is not limited to human beings. Practicing tantra can awaken your body and mind's dormant energy and increase your consciousness. Since energy is the only thing that connects matter and awareness, it is possible to work with it to bring the Shiva consciousness and the Shakti energy together.

It is important to keep nothing aside during this spiritual awakening. Tantra views all circumstances as stepping stones and accepts things as they are. Most tantric techniques are quite effective in helping you let go of anxieties, fears, and other unpleasant feelings while allowing you to feel boundless serenity and love. Given the intensity of tantric practices, you need to commit to them while you are most ready to get the full advantages.

The stages leading up to tantra are yoga and pranayama practice. They play a vital role in producing prana and eliminating harmful substances from the body and psyche. A pure body, mind, and abundant prana create the ideal conditions for Kundalini to rise.

Mantras are essential in tantric practices. Sanskrit is the foundation of most mantras, essential for opening your mind and releasing trapped energy.

Mandalas and yantras play a significant role in tantric ceremonies as well. Tantric practitioners employ yantras as supporting items during meditation. Yantras can assist you in developing mental clarity and identifying energy patterns. Mandalas are essential tools for creating desired mental states. They are symbols that reflect the universe. A tantric could give a mandala particular significance and ask the universe what it wants.

Another potent tantric technique is AntarMouna, often known as inner quiet. It moves methodically through five phases to purge the body and mind of any bad energies that may have accumulated. Tantra doesn't assign blame; instead, it aims to eliminate undesirable components that prevent people from combining their Shiva and Shakti energies.

You can clear your energy centers and begin opening up your mind and integrating with the Supreme Consciousness by using breathing, mantras, and imagery.

It Might Be Frightening And Nerve-Wracking To Talk To Girls.

Feeling anxious while putting oneself out there is normal; it doesn't have to be a challenging experience. We'll give you the skills you need in this book to get by in talks with girls and shine at them.

Be Personable

Being friendly is the most crucial piece of advice when approaching girls. Make eye contact, smile, and appear amiable. Keep your arms relaxed and open while you sit or stand upright. Stay away from crossing your arms because it can make you appear distant. Use a clear, assured voice when speaking. Use your body language to convey your interest in the conversation without being hesitant to do so. If girls sense that you are genuinely interested in what they say, they will be more open to speaking with you.

Show reverence.

It's crucial to treat them with respect when conversing with them. Pay attention to her and convey that you respect her viewpoint. Don't talk over her or interrupt her. Don't force her to say or do anything that makes her uncomfortable; instead, respect her boundaries. It's also critical to show her some consideration for her time. Avoid taking over the conversation or talking too much.

Keep Your Doors Open

Being sincere and upfront about oneself is crucial when speaking with girls. Talk about your feelings and opinions without fear. Ask her about her interests and activities in addition to discussing your own. You and she can establish a stronger bond if you talk to her about your feelings and opinions.

Be Upbeat

It's crucial to maintain your optimistic attitude when speaking with girls. Avoid talking about unfavorable subjects like politics or rumors. Rather, focus on constructive subjects like pastimes, events, and beloved literature. Being upbeat can assist you in fostering a joyful environment where she feels at ease enough to open up to you.

Be Awry

A crucial component of discourse is humor. They highly value Guys who can make girls laugh. It's okay to joke around and make light of yourself. Just be sure that the jokes you tell are tasteful and suitable.

Show Intent

It's critical to express sincere curiosity about what she has to say. Inquire about her life and pay attention to the answers she provides. Express your curiosity by leaving remarks and posing follow-up queries. She will feel more appreciated and that you genuinely care about her.

Defining Non-Binary for Children in Chapter Five

Our sexual anatomy determines our gender at birth; we can be either male or female. When one domino is knocked over, the remaining pieces that make up the line also fall. This initial gender assumption functions similarly to the flip of a domino. However, biological sex is not the same as gender, and gender is not restricted to these two alternatives. Instead, in this instance, gender is the structure, and all of the assumptions and expectations of gender roles and gender expression are the dominoes that fall and can cause the collapse of one's genuine identity. Gender and sex are both mutable. Understanding this can help us see sex and genderless as fixed answers leading to a single conclusion and more as a pendulum or wave.

Some transgender people feel a combination of both or neither gender and don't identify as male or female. We shouldn't be forced to use gendered pronouns like "he" and "him" or "she" and "her" and to fit into the boundaries of a binary, male and female universe.

I know my child is transsexual because of this.

Terms like "gender fluids," "agender," and "genderqueer" fall under the non-binary category. Still, as every person's experience is different, it's best to avoid using labels that someone hasn't permitted us to use. Although I was given the gender of a woman at birth, my identity does not fit neatly into the male or female dichotomy. I use the pronouns "they" and "them," and I identify as non-binary.

1. Honoring Our Distinctions

A change toward a more gender-neutral and egalitarian society is already beginning to emerge. Retailers, toy companies, and clothing manufacturers are revamping their establishments to be more welcoming. Our daughters are learning from us that being intelligent and strong are admirable traits. Our sons are learning from us that processing feelings and having frank conversations about them are healthier options than abusing mental illness or concealing it. Although parents are more tolerant of LGBTQIA people, many are nonetheless afraid of what would happen if one of their children comes out to them. Catching up involves having deep talks with children.

2. Deciding if the person is a boy or a girl.

Never presume or act as though you know the gender of someone a child asks you. Talk to your youngster in an understanding and gender-neutral way by using pronouns like "they" and "them" to convey that you can't know for sure until someone self-identifies. "We don't always know just by looking at someone how they feel inside how they feel," is how Iverson advises answering in response. But what makes you curious about it right now? Stress that it is extremely respectful to not assume someone's gender or pronouns and that we should treat everyone with kindness. I usually use the women's restroom when I'm out in public because there aren't many gender-neutral options. I heard a toddler ask her adult if I was in the correct restroom recently as I was using a stall. This toddler thought I was a boy in a girl's restroom because I carried myself manly. I tensed, having seen too many instances where a parent gave the incorrect answer. However, the mother handled this situation nicely, saying, "I know we are in the right spot, and I am going to trust that person knows they are in the right spot, too."

3. WHAT DO SCHOOLS MEAN BY THE TRUMP ADMINISTRATION'S CHANGE TO TRANSGENDER BATHROOM RIGHTS?

I could have thanked her, but chatting to a stranger in a gendered restroom felt like too much after using one for so long. I wish all parents were that lucid and encouraging. Kids don't have a hard time accepting and adjusting. Parents make assumptions about gender and gender expression that stem from years of bias and taught conceptions. However, parents would find they already have these conversations with their children if they could step back and watch themselves. We teach our children that anyone can wear whatever makes them feel good, work in any field, and use any color. There is a similar explanation for gender identification.

It's critical to instill in our children the belief that, as long as they respect other people's safety, they and others are free to identify, behave, and dress however makes them feel good and healthy. Iverson points out that comfort and safety are not the same things. Being uneasy about something novel does not always translate into danger. The restroom is a prime illustration of this. People are accustomed to bathrooms having separate areas designated for men and women. Still, when other people start urinating where they believe we should, such areas become dangerous for persons who identify as gender nonconforming, transgender, or non-binary.

Iverson continues, "People who are not parallel should be able to use the restroom that ensures their safety and well-being. when some people may feel uncomfortable when we adjust to something new, discomfort is something we can manage as we get used to methods of doing things that are safer and more beneficial for everyone, rather than leaving some people out."

4. Remember: Children Can Comprehend Difficult Ideas

When their young daughter was six, Casey Brown came out as single. Earthy colored acknowledges that their child didn't fully understand personality or orientation then and says that understanding non-twofold was a little confusing but impossible. Brown and their girl used a large piece of paper to write neutral and gendered words. Their daughter understood that the term "young lady" was a better way to describe herself, which helped her to realize that Brown felt the phrases in the objective section best represented him.

Brown's little kid, who is ten years old, says that she understands why people misgender her mom because they have no concept of what it's like to be transsexual. She claims that she always corrects people, but that's because she has to respect her parents' identities.

"If someone asks me, 'Is that your father?' I responded, 'Yes, that is my parent!' Alternatively, if they ask whether it's my mother, I respond, 'Yes, that is my parent!' Thus, I'm changing things without making them seem strange," she explains. We are just a typical family.

Furthermore, that is the main idea. People are people, period. While acknowledging that orientation is and always has been fluid is acceptable, it is not acceptable to violate the safety or presence of another individual. I hope this book has been helpful thus far. Everyone has the right to feel better and to know the truth about sexuality.

How To Be A Bad Boy That Women Want (Not A Dick)

We've all seen movies and TV series about the misunderstood outsider who makes women crazy.

I'm talking about the infamous bad boy image that has captivated women for centuries: Han Solo, Ryan Atwood, and James Dean.

Since that's a terrible foundation for any kind of relationship, I'm here to teach you how to be the bad guy without turning you into a total jackass.

Above all, BE CONFIDENT.

The finest thing you can do to become the naughty boy that girls love is to have confidence.

The confidence issue is that it's a trait that some people possess while others lack it, and other people are very good at pretending to have it.

If you don't think you have a lot of confidence, you should focus on getting more of it. ...or at the very least, pretend to.

Confidence is a part of calmness. By accepting the situation as it is.

It is a good idea to start by decreasing your expectations. We should never project a feeling of helplessness.

A further facet of confidence is resilience.

Being resilient makes it easier to realize that we are in total control of the situation and how we react to it.

Imagine, for example, that you just met a woman you know you like and spilled your drink on her, anyone nearby, or even on you.

No matter what the situation, try not to get scared.

Instead of losing your calm, give her a cloth, offer to clean it up, or let her handle it herself.

Either way, give one apology and then move on. Have perseverance.

You could also make a really smart joke out of it if you spilled it on yourself.

One of the most endearing qualities of the bad boy is his ability to go with the flow. You'll be happier after you acquire this mindset!

It's important to have persistence when you're rejected.

Rejection does happen, but the fear of rejection is far more damaging. Thus, let everything fall off of you.

2. I DO NOT CARE AT ALL.

Once we've regained some confidence, the next thing we need to know about the bad boy is how they play the game of who cares less.

No, I'm not saying you shouldn't care, but girls are drawn to the bad boy because he always seems to be the least concerned.

I'm not asking you to be heartless but to demonstrate your concern for both the woman you're pursuing and other people.

This only means that you care a little bit more about yourself than you do about what other people think of you.

I bet you're wondering why bad boys are such good seducers.

Their "take it or leave it" mentality is to blame for this.

This is a reasonable self-preservation tactic, but it is not a healthy way of life.

Some terrible boys are just insecure about being committed, which makes them aloof from other people. Women also do this.

Being the bad boy also involves locating a girl who doesn't mind becoming committed.

3. PERCEIVE THAT YOU ARE ONE.

You should be at the top if you are single and looking.

You can act distant and with respect.

Nobody likes to waste time, and we definitely don't want to, so if we are clear about our objectives, we may either wait for a response or go on.

Although they may seem like games, courtships, and relationships are not, it would also be prudent for you to either cease playing games entirely or immediately.

4. ENSURE THAT YOU ARE AN EQUAL PART NAUGHTY AND NICE.

Finally, to become the bad boy girls want, balance being naughty and nice.

At all costs, you want to stay away from being a douche canoe.

That won't go far, and you may even receive a swift slap.

However, you also don't want to be unduly courteous. You still want her to follow you around once in a while.

One-sided relationships and chasing women are not acceptable.

If you want to be the bad guy women adore, you must tread carefully between having a good heart and acting like a bad boy.

Being a tough, resilient, self-assured bad boy.

In five simple steps, you can become a wicked boy that girls drool over and the best, most confident version of yourself.

Section I

How to Introduce Sex Education at a Young Age

Learning about sex can be frightening. Even so, God created sex. Seek alternative methods to instill a positive sexuality in your children.

Over the years, one of the most common topics parents ask me is when to start teaching their children about sex education at home. It makes sense that responsible parents would desire unwavering direction on such sensitive topics. As an expert in the treatment of sexual diseases, I have seen the agony caused by misinterpretations and sexual sin, and I believe that the most important lesson we can teach our children is not about God but about sexuality. It is for this reason that it is essential to begin sex education early in life.

Parents often wonder how long they can avoid talking about sex. Hopefully, by the time this chapter ends, you'll be itching to start. Human sexuality is the most precious experience that a husband and wife may share and the most natural thing in the universe.

This is a synopsis of what I would like to communicate to you:

1. Sexuality is essentially the center of our existence as humans. As such, it is our responsibility to instill in our children a thorough awareness of sexuality from an early age.

2. Teaching about sexuality should consider the whole person—spirit, mind, and body—and be grounded in a biblically comprehensive philosophy.

3. If parents wish their children to have a healthy regard and appreciation for the gift of sexuality, they must educate and model the values and precepts that encourage greater sexual health and integrity.

4. Regarding timing, there isn't a better time to begin than the present.

Starting with early sexual education

As I gain more knowledge about God, my passion for the book of Genesis grows. He created a man and a woman who could bear fruit and contribute to his ongoing creation through their unique love for one another. God also knew that a man and a woman would form a special bond through which they would learn to value the differences in each other's physical attributes. The third argument may need to wait until children are mature enough to comprehend it. Still, we can also explain that God created the unity found in married partnerships as a sign and symbol of the interior love of the Trinity and His love for us.

As a result, sexuality imparts to our children at least three essential lessons. Sexual union is necessary for three reasons:

To bear fruit,

To strengthen the bond between a mother and father,

To serve as a symbol of the love the Father, Son, and Holy Spirit have for each other.

As individuals age, sexual education

We can go into greater detail about this first lesson when our children are of age. For example, we may clarify that, particularly for adults and teenagers, wanting to have sex with someone of a different sex is entirely natural and that sex is alluring. The saying "there is a season for everything" and the fact that God is the one who made us want to be healthy male and female representations of ourselves should be emphasized. See 3:1 in Ecclesiastes. This emphasis on timing teaches a child that sex will be appropriate when the moment is right, beginning with a confirmation of sexual desire and developmental maturity.

We'll want to convey the timing clearly and succinctly. It is appropriate for a man and a woman to engage in sexual activity when they are married. All that has to be taught to our younger children is that God intended for men and wives to have sex. Since all sexual practices are meant to prepare youngsters for marriage, we must instill in them a lifelong education about them, including the foreplay that comes before sexual relations.

Cultural and sexual education messages

We can also make teaching moments by emphasizing different cultural messages about sexuality. For example, we cannot protect our children from every lewd sign at the mall or every sultry music played at a restaurant. Before addressing the issues with the erroneous portrayal of sexuality in the media, let us use this opportunity to declare that sexuality is inherently good due to God's loving design. These brief messages will be more impactful if given in a connected and supportive manner. Our teachings must be related to God's love for us and how we can express that love to Him by following.

Teaching children that God's plan is good and Satan's purpose is wicked requires early training. We might talk about good and bad in layman's words early on. We want children to understand how to think about sex from the Bible, not only from our personal experiences or opinions. When children grow older, we shift our approach and teach them how to think.

OTHER ESSENTIAL LESSONS FOR YOUR DAUGHTER IN HER EARLY STAGE

1. Show Her How To Feel Beautiful Within

Instill in your daughter the belief that her true beauty lies not in her outward appearance or attire but in her inner beauty. Stress that genuine beauty originates from within, despite how cheesy this may sound. Assist her in realizing that she is already gorgeous and that trying to be sexy won't make her anymore so. Persuade her that confidence equals beauty and that she is more than just how she looks.

You should be careful about suggesting that she should alter her appearance, though, as research indicates that girls in their preteen and adolescent years are more dissatisfied with their bodies.

Rather than making superficial cosmetic changes to better her appearance, indulge in pleasurable superficial cosmetic changes like learning how to apply cosmetics, getting a new haircut, or exercising. (Ensure that Dad acknowledges her attractiveness as well!)

2. How to Interpret Her Hormone Levels

Assist your daughter in realizing that getting her period marks her body's transition toward becoming a mother and is a beautiful aspect of being a woman. However, be realistic when addressing hormonal changes and let her know that the monthly cycle of hormonal activity can cause her to feel irritable, tired, or melancholy. To be ready for these phases, teach her to correlate them with her cycle. Instruct her on coping mechanisms to prevent hormonal fluctuations from derailing her.

3. Managing Emotions

Girl drama is not at all uncommon. Tell your daughter that she can express herself in a calm and adult way. Teach her how to resolve conflicts with other people.

Show her that she has power over her feelings and behavior. You can better understand your preteen daughter's emotional perspective on life by reading this post about peering inside her thoughts.

4. How She Can Keep Herself Safe

Teach her safety lessons according to her age. Discuss strangers with her when she's in preschool. When she's older, show her how to stay safe if she's at school, at a friend's house, or if she gets approached by someone who acts improperly or makes threats to harm her physically. Give your daughter the information she needs to protect herself both physically and emotionally (if her father is involved, here are three ways he can help, too).

5. How to Take a Stand for Herself

Studies show that schools and parents encourage females to be kind and accommodating. Furthermore, we need to teach our daughters that it's okay to voice their thoughts and beliefs and stand up for themselves, even though we don't want them to go into the world with a grudge and fists up.

Remind your daughter that she can be polite and firm in her expression. Give her the power to say, "I don't like the way you're treating me, so I'm going now," if she feels abused.

6. How To Make Sense-Based Choices

Our daughters' educational and career opportunities are equal to those of men. But unlike men, we have a limited amount of reproductive years. Thus, support your daughter in pursuing her goals while urging her to weigh her options sensibly. She can pursue a career, of course, but she will prioritize her marriage and motherhood if they are important to her.

As someone who married at 38, had her first child at 39, and her second at 40, I can attest that I was unaware that accepting some things meant putting off accepting others.

7. How To Make Sexual Decisions

You need to have a broad conversation with your daughter about sex before you can teach her how to make healthy sexual decisions. Have open discussions about sex to prevent it from becoming a taboo topic. While keeping your family's morals in mind, teach her about sex. As she gets older, tell her the truth about sex and its consequences. You will, regrettably, have to deal with oral sex since many teenage girls view it as a way to have close contact with boys without engaging in "real" sex.

8. How to Appreciate Boys

Instill in your daughter the value of being a person and a woman. For boys, this also holds. Boys are valuable because they are people, not because they are better or more valuable than girls. Assist her in realizing that there is no us (female) vs them (boys) in this world. It is inappropriate to denigrate or ridicule boys based solely on their gender.

Chapter 2: Women's Sexual Education

Sexual education for women is an important and empowering topic that aims to provide women with precise and comprehensive information about their bodies, sexual health, relationships, and reproductive rights.

Systems of Life and Physiology:

Understanding the female contraceptive framework, which encompasses the vagina, uterus, ovaries, fallopian tubes, and bosoms, is a significant component of sexual education for women. Women learn about ovulation, the menstrual cycle, and the role of chemicals in contraceptive health. With the help of this information, women can better understand their bodies and make educated decisions regarding their sexual and contraceptive success.

Feminine Health and the Feminine Cycle: The monthly cycle of women is depicted in sexual education, along with natural interactions, feminine hygiene, and common concerns, including premenstrual syndrome (PMS) and feminine issues. It includes topics including managing women's suffering, tracking menstruation, and dispersing illusions about monthly cycles.

Reproductive Health and Family Planning:

Women are educated about several preventive methods, such as intrauterine devices (IUDs), barrier tactics (such as condoms and stomachs), hormonal contraception (such as anti-conception pills, patches, and infusions), and richness awareness practices. They gather information on the effectiveness, advantages, side effects, and capacity use of contraception to make well-informed decisions for family planning.

Sexual and Reproductive Health:

Women who receive sexual education learn about regenerative health, including pregnancy, childbirth, and postpartum care. Women learn about prenatal care, the importance of maintaining a healthy lifestyle throughout pregnancy, decisions regarding work and transportation, breastfeeding, and the healing process after giving birth. They also receive information regarding common regenerative medical conditions, such as fibroids, endometriosis, and polycystic ovarian syndrome (PCOS).

Contaminations Sent Physically (STIs): Women are instructed on STIs, including how they spread, what to expect, and how to treat them. They learn about a variety of sexually transmitted infections (STIs), including HIV/AIDS, gonorrhea, chlamydia, herpes, and syphilis. Information about regular STI testing, safe sex practices, and where to find appropriate medical care is provided to help women protect both themselves and their partners.

Consent and Audio Relationships:

The importance of consent, boundaries, and communication in sexual relationships is emphasized by sexual training. Women learn about their rights and the importance of providing and receiving enthusiastic, knowledgeable, and forward-thinking consent. They learn to recognize and respond to unfavorable or damaging relationships, enhance self-perception, and foster strong confidence.

Joy and intimacy in sex:

A comprehensive sexual education curriculum acknowledges the importance of intimacy and pleasure in the sexual realm. It gets people talking about the joys of femininity, climax, masturbation, and many sexual directions. Women learn about their energy bodies, explore their desires, and have strong opinions about their sexuality.

Intellectual Liberties and Enhancement:

For women, sexual education aims to empower them by increasing awareness of their regenerative rights. It informs women about their rights to family planning services, safe and legal early abortion, and full medical coverage. It also discusses social and cultural aspects that could affect women's decisions about contraception and advocates for regenerative fairness.

Cybersecurity and Computer-Based Learning:

Because women must use technology, sexual education for them includes:

Teaching them about online safety

Consenting in technologically advanced environments

Responsible use of the Internet for entertainment

Women learn about protecting their online privacy, responding to cyberbullies, and identifying and reporting instances of abuse or badgering on the Internet.

Interconnectedness and Inclusivity:

A comprehensive program for sexual education recognizes and responds to the diverse experiences and needs of women from all backgrounds, including those who belong to different racial groups, identities, faiths, and sexual orientations.

LGBTQ+ Inclusion:

An all-encompassing sexual education curriculum recognizes and tackles the unique needs and experiences of women who identify as lesbian, gay, transgender, queer, or queer-related (LGBTQ+). It provides information about sexual orientation, personality traits, and sexual direction, as well as the specific health issues and resources available to LGBTQ+ individuals. This promotes understanding, support, and validation of diverse sexual orientations and directions.

Self-awareness and Self-assurance:

Sexual education emphasizes how important it is for women to have a positive self-image and confidence. It frequently results in media effects, absurd excellence standards, and societal tensions that may have an impact on how women view their bodies and sexuality.

Delight-Based Methodology:

Comprehensive sexual education programs adopt a pleasure-based methodology that acknowledges and validates women's pleasure and desires in the sexual domain. It provides information on erogenous zones, sexual responses, and methods for enhancing pleasure during sex. By promoting a pleasurable and fulfilling sexual experience, women are empowered to explore their desires, express their needs, and concentrate on their enjoyment in intimate relationships.

Talk About Sex And Puberty Begins At Home.

The best persons to teach a child about sexuality are the ones who are closest to him at home. Anyone can learn the principles of reproduction in an hour or two (or read them in any number of reference books).

But since you are in the best position to do so, you are the most qualified to provide this knowledge with the required context and perspective over several years.

Although there aren't any strict standards for finishing this work, bear the following in mind:

1. Not All Facts Are Negative

It does not diminish a child's innocence to teach him about reproduction, including details about sex. Innocence is determined by attitude rather than information. A school-age child maintains his innocence by understanding the details of sex but yet seeing it as an act that, under the right conditions, may both express love and spark a new life. However, a young child may already possess a corrupt attitude if he has had sex in an abusive, humiliating, or demeaning environment.

2. Exercise patience

Don't hold off on teaching your child everything you know about sex until after one lengthy, intense session. You run the risk of either giving the child more knowledge than he can manage or waiting until it's too late by doing this. Instead, divulge information in negotiations for several years. The same principle can be used in every other area of life. Discussions concerning faith, values, responsibilities, relationships, and money management must be ongoing and multiple. Some subjects, like talking about puberty and sex, are too important to handle in a single conversation.

3. Necessary yet not necessary

You will often be dispersing information according to need-to-know. Your five-year-old will likely want to know how Aunt Susie's baby will get out. However, your child may not ask how the baby got there. Besides, there's no reason to discuss the issue at that moment. However, you will have to initiate the conversation on reproduction if you and your ten-year-old haven't yet covered it. She needs information from more knowledgeable and reliable sources.

FIRST CHAPTER: THE LUST LANGUAGE
DIRTY TALK: WHAT IS IT?

In its most basic form, dirty talk refers to sexy statements meant to arouse your partner's desire for sex. Deceptive language functions by stimulating one's imagination in this way, building your partner's arousal earlier on during sexual activity. To fulfill its purpose, dirty language stimulates your ideal partner's real senses (sound, touch, sight, and so on) and subsequently sets off the correct reaction in him or her. While they're in the throes of passionate passion, couples use dirty talk to express what they need from one another.

What types of conversations are these?

supple core

Another name for this is "love words." The vocabulary used in delicate center dirty talking isn't dirty. Or perhaps they are meant to sound cozy, comforting, and even affectionate. Engaging your partner in conversation about your feelings and eliciting a response from them is the purpose of the delicate center of dirty talk. A great way to introduce the no-nonsense love language into the conversation is to use delicate center filthy talk. Use it to set up your partner, gauge how he feels about the sexual conversation, and find out what boundaries he is willing to cross.

Models:

"You're the most sizzling thing I've at any point seen."

"I need to hold you so gravely."

"I love the stuff that you do with your fingers."

"Child, I've never felt so good."

These can sound like lackluster statements. Therefore, regulating how you state softcore terms is important to having them sound utterly unclean. Everything is based on the feelings you want your partner to have and the reaction you want to get out of him/her. If you want your message to sound passionate and assertive, speak in a gruff voice or through clenched teeth as if you're fighting to keep yourself from hitting your partner. Accept a gentle tone and speak in a whisper if you must sound pensive and venerating.

The way you carry yourself visually also has a big impact on how important the message is. When your lover's privates are being inspected rather than their face, a sweet middle expression like "You're the most sizzling thing I've ever seen." can easily turn into blunt, nasty discourse.

Similarly, the context can affect how you interpret what you say. Saying, "Child, I've never felt so great," is more confrontational when a man is having sex with a woman, and he is expressing something deep inside of her. When he says the same words when in a lip-lock during foreplay, they will generally have a gentler center. Again, the same words will mean something different when he says them after sex and remembers that he and his partner are cuddling. "Child, I've never felt so great." used to be uplifting, but now it's comforting.

ardent

If limited to diplomatic, center-of-the-mouth banter, no-nonsense expressions will typically be more direct and, most of the time, seem impolite. The goal is to elicit a bodily response rather than an enthusiastic one. The straightforward, nasty speech appeals to the primal urge—perhaps even the beastly nature. They inspire the most modest people to unleash their inner monsters. Simple language encourages people to let go of their inhibitions as soon as they enter a room, to embrace happiness without hesitation, and to speak freely.

Swear words may be used during serious, nasty conversations. Is it possible for profanity to suddenly become sexy? When someone who doesn't typically use profanity ends up using it when making love, it appears they are losing control. It makes your partner think that the sex is okay to the extent that you are unsure of how to describe it, and as a result, you end up using vulgar terminology. Bad-to-the-bone language is a common tool used by couples to push boundaries and make sexual pretending seem more realistic. In reality, we all play different roles (such as the adoring mother, the wonderful spouse, the kind neighbor, the skilled worker, and so on), and social norms constrain these personalities. Saying things you wouldn't normally say when portraying these personalities gives you the confidence to drop all those roles and dive right into becoming an energizing being with a boundless capacity for delight.

Talking about dirty things also serves as a shared mystery between partners, strengthening your bond. The best thing about overtly sexual language is that it sounds real and unadulterated. The blatant stupidity demonstrates to your partner that the statements originate deep within you. Talking nasty in public gives your partner the impression that they have access to a side of you that you only occasionally reveal.

www.ingramcontent.com/pod-product-compliance
Lightning Source LLC
Chambersburg PA
CBHW052138110526
44591CB00012B/1772